Aphorisms

Kafka in Zürau, circa 1917–18

FRANZ KAFKA

Aphorisms

Translated from the German by
WILLA AND EDWIN MUIR AND
BY MICHAEL HOFMANN

Foreword by
DANIEL FRANK

Schocken Books

NEW YORK

Compilation copyright © 2015 by Schocken Books,
a division of Penguin Random House LLC

Foreword copyright © 2015 by Daniel Frank

All rights reserved. Published in the United States by Schocken
Books, a division of Penguin Random House LLC, New York,
and distributed in Canada by Random House of Canada,
a division of Penguin Random House Ltd., Toronto. Portions
of this work originally appeared in *The Great Wall of China:
Stories and Reflections,* copyright © 1946 by Schocken Books,
a division of Penguin Random House LLC and in
The Zürau Aphorisms of Franz Kafka, copyright © 2006 by
Schocken Books, a division of Penguin Random House LLC

Schocken Books and colophon are registered trademarks of
Penguin Random House LLC.

Library of Congress Cataloging-in-Publication Data
Kafka, Franz, 1883–1924, author.
[Aphorisms. Selections. English]
Aphorisms / Franz Kafka; Translated from the German by
Willa and Edwin Muir and by Michael Hofmann;
Foreword by Daniel Frank.
pages   cm.
ISBN 978-0-8052-1265-5 (hardback).
ISBN 978-0-8052-4336-9 (eBook).
1. Kafka, Franz, 1883–1924—Quotations.   2. Aphorisms and
apothegms.   I. Title.
PT2621.A26A2 2015   838'.91207—dc23
2015025049

www.schocken.com

Jacket design by Peter Mendelsund

Printed in the United States of America

First Edition

4   6   8   9   7   5

CONTENTS

THE AFTERLIFE OF FRAGMENTS

Foreword by Daniel Frank

I

The word *aphorism* comes from the Greek αφοριζειν, which means to define. The Greek word is a compound of the preposition απο—apart from—and όριζειυ—to divide or separate from as a boundary and from which we get the word *horizon*. An aphorism suggests the distance that allows one to see the horizon. The horizon is an early experience of a boundary. A definition determines the boundary of a word, its use and meaning. Meaning and use are often aligned, but usage can be more flexible, so we speak of proper or improper use. Improper use may alter a word's meaning, shifting the terrain of its use.

Definitions offer boundaries for words, while aphorisms use words to consider the nature of boundaries—how or where they arise or are drawn. Aphorisms recast boundaries as distinctions, transform what may be visible or literal into something abstract or metaphoric, while preserving the intersection of these aspects. (1)

II

We create boundaries by drawing lines, constructing paths, building walls. These are often the subject of aphorisms. One of the earliest examples is Heraclitus's remark that the road up and down is one and the same. Heraclitus's line is a paradox—the beginning of a road is also its end. The beginning and the end are one and the same. T. S. Eliot used Heraclitus's fragments as an epigraph for the *Four Quartets,* his effort to explore that paradox:

> *What we call the beginning is often the end*
> *And to make an end is to make a beginning*
> *("Little Gidding")*

III

Kafka opens the sequence of Zürau aphorisms by drawing an analogy between a path and a rope:

> The true path is along a rope, not a rope suspended way up in the air, but rather only just

over the ground. It serves more like a tripwire than a tightrope.

A path connects one place to another, but it also measures the distance that separates two places. A line at once joins two points and keeps them apart. This fusion between opposed meanings can also be found in the English word *cleave,* which means both to break apart and to join together.

It is not only a matter of joining two opposed meanings but of finding the balance that holds those opposed meanings together. Kafka's very formulation is precise—"it seems more like a tripwire than a tightrope." A tightrope requires balance, a tripwire causes one to lose balance. For Kafka, the tension required for balance also undermines the possibility of balance.

Here is Kafka musing again on centripetal and centrifugal forces:

As firmly as a hand holding a stone. Held, however so firmly, merely so that it can be flung a greater distance.

And then, he concludes by suggesting a return:

But there is a path even to that distance. (21)

An aphorism is an acrobatic act that allows us to let go of what's been caught—and the prospect of releasing is the point we need to reach. Or, in Kafka's words:

> From a certain point there is no turning back. That is the point that must be reached. (5)

But Kafka himself turns back on that possibility in one of his most famous aphorisms:

> Man found the Archimedean point, but he used it against himself; it seems that he was permitted to find it only under that condition.

IV

Heraclitus is aware of the tension between reaching and turning back—and wants to suggest that in the equipoise of the distance, the need to hold apart and bring together two points, lies the possibility of harmony:

> There is a harmony in the turning back, like that of the bow and lyre.

V

One of Kafka's aphorisms works as a definition of a distinction: "The world is only ever a constructed world." (54) He elaborates this statement a little later: "The fact that the only world is a constructed world takes away hope and gives us certainty" (62). The word *constructed* suggests a sense of arbitrariness, that significance itself is constructed, and so it can also be deconstructed or destroyed. Aphorisms offer distinctions that allow us to determine what we see or can't see, between what is visible or invisible, divisible or indivisible. Without distinctions, we cannot see. But if we insist that our distinctions exist beyond the particular moment of what we've seen, we risk transforming them into the bars of a cage which imprison us. In the sequence of aphorisms called HE, Kafka writes: "The din of the world streams out and in through the bars. The prisoner was really free, he could simply have left the cage, the bars were yards apart, he was not even a prisoner." In the Zürau sequence, Kafka refines that extended metaphor to a single image: "A cage went in search of a bird." (16)

VI

Q: When does a constructed world become a
   cage?
A: The constructed world is a cage.

VII

One can find an analogy to Kafka's "constructed world"
in Heraclitus's phrase, ήθος ανϱώπωι, which is often
translated as "human character," but that phrase overlooks the original meaning of ήθος as *haunt* or *abode,*
a place that, by our capacity to adapt, we transform
into a habitable dwelling, a place to which we become
accustomed. Heraclitus's most famous aphorism, ήθος
ανϱώπωι δαίμων, might be constructed as, "the
human ability to adapt does not belong to us," or
"what allows us to be human is something daemonic."
Kafka suggests analogous tension in the German word
sein, which signifies both "to be there" and "to belong
to Him." (46)

   Kafka also sees the tension between the human and
the daemonic as one between the self and the world:
"in the struggle between yourself and the world hold
the world's coat." (52)

VIII

Borges once suggested, in a piece called "Kafka and his Precursors," that every writer creates his own precursors.

IX

A dialogue:

> HERACLITUS: Nature likes to hide.
>
> KAFKA: Man cannot live without a steady faith in something indestructible within him, though both the faith and the indestructible thing may remain permanently concealed from him. (50)
>
> HERACLITUS: The Lord whose oracle is at Delphi neither speaks plainly nor conceals but indicates by signs.
>
> KAFKA: Language can only be used very obliquely of things about the physical world since all it knows to do—according to the nature of the physical world—is to treat of ownership and its relations. (57)

X

Aphorisms disclose aspects of what we may or may not be able to see. We may not even recognize the direction in which we are pointed when we catch sight of the continually shifting line between being awake and being asleep.

> The same person has perceptions that, for all their difference, have the same object which leads one to infer that there are different subjects contained within one and the same person. (72)

Keats once wrote, "I have a habitual feeling of my real life having passed and that I am leading a posthumous existence." Aphorisms are postscripts of that real life; they record breaches in the boundaries that are at once permanent and transient, fragments of what we once saw and hope to see again.

THE ZÜRAU APHORISMS

———

I

The true path is along a rope, not a rope suspended way up in the air, but rather only just over the ground. It seems more like a tripwire than a tightrope.

All human errors stem from impatience, a premature breaking off of a methodical approach, an ostensible pinning down of an ostensible object.

3

There are two cardinal human vices, from which all the others derive their being: impatience and carelessness. Impatience got people evicted from Paradise; carelessness kept them from making their way back there. Or perhaps there is only one cardinal vice: impatience. Impatience got people evicted, and impatience kept them from making their way back.*

---

* Editor's note: Asterisks indicate aphorisms that were crossed out by Kafka on his original onionskin sheets.

4

Many of the shades of the departed busy themselves entirely with lapping at the waters of the Acheron, because it comes from us and still carries the salt tang of our seas. This causes the river to coil with revulsion, and even to reverse its course, and so to wash the dead back to life. They are perfectly happy, and sing choruses of gratitude, and caress the indignant river.

5

From a certain point on, there is no more turning back. That is the point that must be reached.

The decisive moment of human development is continually at hand. This is why those movements of revolutionary thought that declare everything preceding to be an irrelevance are correct—because as yet nothing has happened.

7

One of the most effective seductions of Evil is the call to struggle. It's like the struggle with women, which ends up in bed.

A smelly bitch that has brought forth plenty of young, already rotting in places, but that to me in my childhood meant everything, who continually follow me faithfully everywhere, whom I am quite incapable of disciplining, but before whom I shrink back, step by step, shying away from her breath, and who will end up—unless I decide otherwise—forcing me into a corner that I can already see, there to decompose fully and utterly on me and with me, until finally—is it a distinction?—the pus- and worm-ravaged flesh of her tongue laps at my hand.

A. is terribly puffed up, he considers himself very advanced in goodness, since he feels himself magnetically attracting to himself an ever greater array of temptations, from quarters with which he was previously wholly unacquainted. The true explanation for his condition, however, is that a great devil has taken up residence within him, and an endless stream of smaller devils and deviltons are coming to offer the great one their services.

The variety of views that one may have, say, of an apple: the view of the small boy who has to crane his neck for a glimpse of the apple on the table, and the view of the master of the house who picks up the apple and hands it to a guest.

13

A first indication of glimmering understanding is the desire to die. This life seems unendurable, another unreachable. One no longer feels ashamed of wanting to die; one petitions to be moved from one's old cell, which one hates, into a new one, which one will come to hate. A last vestige of belief is involved here, too, for during the move might not the prison governor by chance walk down the passage, see the prisoner, and say: "Don't lock this man up again. He's coming with me."

If you were walking across a plain, felt every desire
to walk, and yet found yourself going backward, it
would be a cause for despair; but as you are in fact
scaling a steep precipice, as sheer in front of you as
you are from the ground, then your backward move-
ment can be caused only by the terrain, and you would
be wrong to despair.*

Like a path in autumn: no sooner is it cleared than it is once again littered with fallen leaves.

16

A cage went in search of a bird.

———

I have never been here before: my breath comes differently, the sun is outshone by a star beside it.

If it had been possible to build the Tower of Babel without having to climb it, that would have been sanctioned.

———

Don't let Evil convince you you could keep any secrets from it.

Leopards break into the temple and drink all the sacrificial vessels dry; it keeps happening; in the end, it can be calculated in advance and is incorporated into the ritual.

As firmly as a hand holding a stone. Held, however, so firmly, merely so that it can be flung a greater distance. But there is a path even to that distance.

You are the exercise, the task. No student far and wide.

From the true opponent, a limitless courage flows into you.

Grasp the good fortune that the ground on which you stand cannot be any bigger than the two feet planted on it.

How is it possible to rejoice in the world except by fleeing to it?

There are innumerable hiding places and only one salvation, but the possibilities of salvation are as numerous as the hiding places.*

. . .

There is a destination but no way there; what we refer to as way is hesitation.

We are instructed to do the negative; the positive is already within us.

Once we have taken Evil into ourselves, it no longer insists that we believe in it.

The reservations with which you take Evil into yourself are not yours, but those of Evil.

· · ·

The animal twists the whip out of its master's grip and whips itself to become its own master—not knowing that this is only a fantasy, produced by a new knot in the master's whiplash.

Goodness is in a certain sense comfortless.*

I do not strive for self-mastery. Self-mastery is the desire—within the endless emanations of my intellectual life—to be effective at a certain radius. But if I am made to describe circles around me, then I had better do it without action: merely contemplating the whole extraordinary complex and taking nothing away with me but the strength that such an aspect—*e contrario*—would give me.

The crows like to insist a single crow is enough to destroy heaven. This is incontestably true, but it says nothing about heaven, because heaven is just another way of saying: the impossibility of crows.

33

Martyrs do not underestimate the body, they allow it to be hoisted up onto the cross. In that way they are like their enemies.

His exhaustion is that of the gladiator after the combat; his labor was the whitewashing of a corner of the wall in his office.

35

There is no possessing, only an existing, only an existing that yearns for its final breath, for asphyxiation.

Earlier, I didn't understand why I got no answer to my question, today I don't understand how I presumed to ask a question. But then I didn't presume, I only asked.

His answer to the accusation that he might possess something but didn't exist, consisted of trembling and heart palpitations.

A man was astounded by the ease of the path of eternity; it was because he took it downhill, at a run.

It is not possible to pay Evil in installments—and still we always try.

. . .

It is conceivable that Alexander the Great—for all the military successes of his youth, for all the excellence of the army he trained, for all the desire he felt in himself to change the world—might have stopped at the Hellespont, and never crossed it, and not out of fear, not out of indecisiveness, not out of weakness of will, but from heavy legs.

The road is endless, there are no shortcuts and no detours, and yet everyone brings to it his own child-ish haste. "You must walk this ell of ground, too, you won't be spared it."

40

It's only our notion of time that allows us to speak of the Last Judgment, in fact it's a Court Martial.*

The disproportion of the world seems fortunately to be merely numerical.*

42

To let one's hate- and disgust-filled head slump onto one's chest.

The dogs are still playing in the yard, but the quarry will not escape them, never mind how fast it is running through the forest already.

44

___

You have girded your loins in a most laughable way
for this world.

45

The more horses you put to, the faster your progress—
not of course in the removal of the cornerstone from
the foundations, which is impossible, but in the tear-
ing of the harness, and your resultant riding cheerfully
off into space.

46

The German word *sein* signifies both "to be there" and "to belong to Him."

They were offered the choice between being kings and being royal envoys. Like children, they all wanted to be envoys. This is why there are so many envoys chasing through the world, shouting—for the want of kings—the most idiotic messages to one another. They would willingly end their miserable lives, but because of their oaths of duty, they don't dare to.

48

Belief in progress doesn't mean belief in progress that has already occurred. That would not require belief.

49

A. is a virtuoso, and Heaven is his witness.

50

A man cannot live without a steady faith in something indestructible within him, though both the faith and the indestructible thing may remain permanently concealed from him. One of the forms of this concealment is the belief in a personal god.

It took the intercession of the serpent: Evil can seduce a man, but not become human.*

52

In the struggle between yourself and the world, hold the world's coat.

53

It is wrong to cheat, even if it is the world of its victory.

54

The world is only ever a constructed world; what we call the sensual world is Evil in the constructed world, and what we call Evil is only a fleeting necessity in our eternal development.

. . .

With a very strong light, one can make the world disappear. Before weak eyes it will become solid; before still weaker eyes, it will acquire fists; and to eyes yet weaker, it will be embarrassed and punch the face of anyone who dares to look at it.

Everything is deception: the question is whether to seek the least amount of deception, or the mean, or to seek out the highest. In the first instance, you will cheat goodness by making it too easy to acquire, and Evil by imposing too unfavorable conditions on it. In the second instance, you cheat goodness by failing to strive for it in this earthly life. In the third instance, you cheat goodness by removing yourself from it as far as you can, and Evil by maximizing it in a bid to reduce its impact. Accordingly, the second option is the one to go for, because you always cheat goodness, but—in this case at least, or so it would seem—not Evil.

56

There are questions we could never get past, were it not that we are freed of them by nature.

Language can be used only very obliquely of things outside the physical world, not even metaphorically, since all it knows to do—according to the nature of the physical world—is to treat of ownership and its relations.

58

The way to tell fewest lies is to tell fewest lies, not to give oneself the fewest opportunities of telling lies.*

To its own way of seeing, a wooden stair moder-
ately hollowed out by people's footfalls is just some
knocked-together article of wood.*

60

Whoever renounces the world must love humanity, because he is also renouncing their world. Accordingly, he will begin to have a true sense of human nature, which is incapable of anything but being loved—assuming, that is, that one is on the same footing as it.

Whoever in this world loves his neighbor does just as much and just as little wrong as who in this world loves himself. Remains the question whether the former is possible.*

62

The fact that the only world is a constructed world takes away hope and gives us certainty.

63

Our art is an art that is dazzled by truth: the light shed on the rapidly fleeing grimace is true—nothing else is.

The Expulsion from Paradise is eternal in its principal aspect: this makes it irrevocable, and our living in this world inevitable, but the eternal nature of the process has the effect that not only could we remain forever in Paradise, but that we are currently there, whether we know it or not.

He is a free and secure citizen of the world because he is on a chain that is long enough to allow him access to all parts of the earth, and yet not so long that he could be swept over the edge of it. At the same time he is also a free and secure citizen of heaven because he is also attached to a similar heavenly chain. If he wants to go to earth, the heavenly manacles will throttle him, if he wants to go to heaven, the earthly manacles will. But for all that, all possibilities are open to him, as he is well aware, yes, he even refuses to believe the whole thing is predicated on a mistake going back to the time of his first enchainment.

67

He runs after the facts like someone learning to skate,
who furthermore practices where it is dangerous and
has been forbidden.

68

Is there anything as blithe as believing in one's own household god!

Theoretically, there is one consummate possibility of felicity: to believe in the indestructible in oneself, and then not to go looking for it.

The indestructible is one thing; at one and the same time it is each individual, and it is something common to all; hence the uniquely indissoluble connection among mankind.

72

The same person has perceptions that, for all their differences, have the same object, which leads one to infer that there are different subjects contained within one and the same person.*

73

He scavenges the leftovers from his own table; that makes him better fed than the others for a little while, but he also forgets how to eat at table; and so the supply of leftovers dries up.

74

If what was supposed to be destroyed in Paradise was destructible, then it can't have been decisive; however, if it was indestructible, then we are living in a false belief.

Test yourself against mankind. It teaches the doubter to doubt and the believer to believe.*

The feeling: "I'm not dropping anchor here," and straightaway the feeling of the sustaining sea-swell around one.

. . .

A reversal. Lurking, fretful, hoping, the answer creeps around the question, peers despairingly in its averted face, follows it on its most abstruse journeys—that is, those that have least to do with the answer.

Dealings with people bring about self-scrutiny.

The spirit only becomes free at the point where it ceases to be invoked as a support.

79

Sexual love deceives us as to heavenly love; were it alone, it would not be able to do so, but containing within itself, unknowingly, a germ of heavenly love, it can.

80

————

The truth is indivisible and is therefore incapable of recognizing itself; whatever claims to recognize it must therefore be a lie.*

No one can crave what truly harms him. If in the case of some individuals things have that appearance—and perhaps they always do—the explanation is that someone within the person is demanding something useful to himself but very damaging to a second person, who has been brought along partly to give his opinion on the matter. If the man had taken the part of the second person from the outset, and not just when the time came to make a decision, then the first person would have been suppressed, and with it the craving.

82

Why do we harp on about Original Sin? It wasn't on its account that we were expelled from Paradise, but because of the Tree of Life, lest we eat of its fruit.

83

___

We are sinful, not only because we have eaten of the Tree of Knowledge, but also because we have not yet eaten of the Tree of Life. The condition in which we find ourselves is sinful, guilt or no guilt.

84

We were created to live in Paradise, and Paradise was designed to serve us. Our designation has been changed; we are not told whether this has happened to Paradise as well.

Evil is an emanation of human consciousness at certain transitional points. It is not really the physical world that is illusion, but the Evil of it, which to our eyes constitutes, admittedly, the physical world.

Ever since Original Sin, we are basically all alike in our ability to know Good and Evil; even so, this is where we seek a particular advantage. Actually, it's only after knowledge that the real differences begin. The appearance to the contrary is provoked in the following way: No one can be satisfied with understanding alone but must make an effort to act in accordance with it. He lacks the strength to do so; therefore he must destroy himself, even at the risk of not receiving the necessary strength; it is simply that he has no option other than to undertake this final effort. (This is the meaning of the penalty of death for eating of the Tree of Knowledge; it may also be the original meaning of natural death.) The effort is daunting; one would rather reverse the original knowledge of Good and Evil; (the term "Original Sin" refers to this fear) but what was done cannot be undone, only muddied. To this end motivations appear. The entire world is full of them—

yes, the whole visible world may be nothing more than a motivation of a man wanting to rest for a moment. An attempt to forge the fact of knowledge, to make of the knowledge an end in itself.

———

A faith like an ax. As heavy, as light.

Death is ahead of us, say in the way in our classrooms we had a picture of Alexander the Great in battle. What must be done is by our actions to blot out or obscure the picture, in our lifetimes.

Two alternatives: either to make oneself infinitesimally small, or to be so. The former is perfection and hence inaction; the latter a beginning and therefore action.*

To avoid the solecism: Whatever is to be entirely destroyed must first be held very firmly; if something crumbles, it crumbles, but resists destruction.*

92

—————

The first case of idolatry was surely fear of things, and therefore also fear of the necessity of things, and therefore also of responsibility for them. This responsibility seemed so vast that people didn't even dare to lay it at the feet of a single divine being, because the intervention of one such being would not sufficiently lighten the weight of human responsibility, the negotiation with one being would have remained too much stained with the responsibility, and therefore each thing was given the responsibility for itself, or more, the things were also given a measure of responsibility for the human.

93

No psychology ever again!*

94

Two tasks of the beginning of life: to keep reducing your circle, and to keep making sure you're not hiding somewhere outside it.

Evil is sometimes like a tool in your hand, recognized or unrecognized, you are able, if you have the will to do it, to set it aside, without being opposed.

The joys of this life are not *its* joys, but *our* fear of climbing into a higher life; the torments of this life are not its torments, but our self-torment on account of this fear.

Only here is suffering really suffering. Not in the way that those who suffer here are to be ennobled in some other world for their suffering, but that what passes for suffering in this world is, in another world, without any change and merely without its contrariety, bliss.

98

The conception of the infinite plenitude and expanse
of the universe is the result of taking to an extreme
a combination of strenuous creativity and free contemplation.

How much more oppressive than the most implacable conviction of our current state of sin is even the feeblest contemplation of the once eternal justification for our ephemerality. Only the strength fixed in bearing the second conviction—which in its purity completely encloses the first—is the measure of faith.

. . .

There are some who assume that next to the great original deception, another, smaller deception was practiced specifically for them. It's as if, when a romantic comedy is performed on stage, the actress, in addition to the lying smile for her beloved, keeps a further, particularly cunning smile for a certain spectator in Row Z. That is going too far.

100

———

It is possible to know of the devilish but not to believe in it, because there is no more devilishness than exists anyway.

Sin always comes openly, and in a form apprehensible to the senses. It walks on its roots and doesn't need to be plucked out of the ground.

All the sufferings we occasion we must also suffer. We don't all share one body, but we do share growth, and that leads us through all pain, whether in this form or that. As the child grows through all its phases and becomes old and dies (and every stage seems unattainable to those before, whether from desire or from dread), so we develop (no less connected to others than to ourselves) through all the sufferings of the world. There is in this context no room for justice, and not for fear of suffering either, or for the presentation of suffering as merit.

You can withdraw from the sufferings of the world—
that possibility is open to you and accords with your
nature—but perhaps that withdrawal is the only suffering you might be able to avoid.

Man has free will, and of three sorts:

First he was free when he wanted this life; now admittedly he cannot take back his decision, because he is no longer the one who wanted it then, he must do his own will then by living.

Second he is free inasmuch as he can choose the pace and the course of his life.

Third he is free in that as the person he will one day be, he has the will to go through life under any condition and so come to himself, on some path of his own choosing, albeit sufficiently labyrinthine that it leaves no little spot of life untouched.

This is the triple nature of free will, but being simultaneous, it is also single, and is in fact so utterly single that it has no room for a will at all, whether free or unfree.

The seductiveness of this world and the sign that warrants its transitoriness are one and the same. And rightly so, because only in this way can the world seduce us, and accord with the truth. The grievous thing is that after falling victim to the seduction, we forget the warranty, and so the Good has led us into Evil, the woman's smile has led us into bed with her.

106

Humility gives everyone, even the lonely and the desperate, his strongest tie to his fellow men. Immediately and spontaneously, too, albeit only if the humility is complete and lasting. It does so because it is the language of prayer and is both worship and tie. The relationship to one's fellow man is the relationship of prayer; the relationship to oneself is the relationship of striving; out of prayer is drawn the strength with which to strive.

.   .   .

Can you know anything that is not deception? Once deception was destroyed, you wouldn't be able to look, at the risk of turning into a pillar of salt.

Everyone is very friendly to A., in roughly the way one might seek to protect an excellent billiard cue even from good players, until the great one comes along, takes a good look at the table, will tolerate no precocious mistakes, and then, when he starts playing, rampages in the wildest way.

108

_____

"And then he went back to his job, as though nothing had happened." A sentence that strikes one as familiar from any number of old stories—though it might not have appeared in any of them.

"It cannot be claimed that we are lacking in belief. The mere fact of our being alive is an inexhaustible font of belief."

"The fact of our being alive a font of belief? But what else can we do but live?"

"It's in that 'what else' that the immense force of belief resides: it is the exclusion that gives it its form."

. . .

It isn't necessary that you leave home. Sit at your desk and listen. Don't even listen, just wait. Don't wait, be still and alone. The whole world will offer itself to you to be unmasked, it can do no other, it will writhe before you in ecstasy.

"He"

Notes from the Year 1920

He is never quite ready for any contingency, yet he cannot even blame himself for that, for when in this life, which insists so mercilessly that we must be ready at every moment, can one ever find time in which to make oneself ready? and even if there were time how can one make ready before knowing the task; in other words, can one ever be equal to a natural task, a spontaneous task that has not merely been artificially concocted? So he has long since fallen under the wheels; a contingency for which, strangely enough, but also comfortingly enough, he was least ready of all.

All that he does seems to him, it is true, extraordinarily new, but also, because of the incredible spate of new things, extraordinarily amateurish, indeed scarcely tolerable, incapable of becoming history, breaking short the chain of the generations, cutting off for the first time at its most profound source the music of the world, which before him could at least be divined.

Sometimes in his arrogance he has more anxiety for the world than for himself.

He could have resigned himself to a prison. To end as a prisoner—that could be a life's ambition. But it was a barred cage that he was in. Calmly and insolently, as if at home, the din of the world streamed out and in through the bars, the prisoner was really free, he could take part in everything, nothing that went on outside escaped him, he could simply have left the cage, the bars were yards apart, he was not even a prisoner.

He has the feeling that merely by being alive he is blocking his own way. From this sense of hindrance, in turn, he deduces the proof that he is alive.

The bony structure of his own forehead blocks his way; he batters himself bloody against his own forehead.

He feels imprisoned on this earth, he feels constricted; the melancholy, the impotence, the sicknesses, the feverish fancies of the captive afflict him; no comfort can comfort him, since it is merely comfort, gentle head-splitting comfort glozing the brutal fact of imprisonment. But if he is asked what he actually wants he cannot reply, for—that is one of his strongest proofs—he has no conception of freedom.

Franz Kafka

Some deny the existence of misery by pointing to the sun; he denies the existence of the sun by pointing to misery.

The sluggish, self-torturing, wavelike motion of all life, whether of other life or his own, which often seems to stagnate for a long time but in reality never ceases, tortures him because it brings with it the never-ceasing compulsion to think. Sometimes it seems to him that this torture heralds events. When he hears that a friend is awaiting the birth of a child he recognizes that in thought he has already suffered for that birth.

He sees in two ways: the first is a calm contemplation, consideration, investigation, an overflow of life inevitably involving a certain sensation of comfort. The possible manifestations of this process are infinite, for though even a woodlouse needs a relatively large crevice in which to accommodate itself, no space whatever is required for such labors; even where not the smallest crack can be found they may exist in tens of thousands, mutually interpenetrating one another. That is the first stage. The second is the moment when he is called upon to render an account of all this, finds himself incapable of uttering a sound, is flung back again on contemplation, etc., but now, knowing the hopelessness of it, can no longer dabble about in it, and so makes his body heavy and sinks with a curse.

This is the problem: Many years ago I sat one day, in a sad enough mood, on the slopes of the Laurenziberg. I went over the wishes that I wanted to realize in life. I found that the most important or the most delightful was the wish to attain a view of life (and—this was necessarily bound up with it—to convince others of it in writing), in which life, while still retaining its natural full-bodied rise and fall, would simultaneously be recognized no less clearly as a nothing, a dream, a dim hovering. A beautiful wish, perhaps, if I had wished it rightly. Considered as a wish, somewhat as if one were to hammer together a table with painful and methodical technical efficiency, and simultaneously do nothing at all, and not in such a way that people could say: "Hammering a table together is nothing to him," but rather, "Hammering a table together is really hammering a table together to him, but at the same time it is nothing," whereby certainly the hammering would have become still bolder, still surer, still more real and, if you will, still more senseless.

But he could not wish in this fashion, for his wish was not a wish, but only a vindication of nothingness, a justification of non-entity, a touch of animation which he wanted to lend to non-entity, in which at that time he had scarcely taken his first few conscious steps, but which he already felt as his element. It was a sort of farewell that he took from the illusive world of youth; although youth had never directly deceived him, but only caused him to be deceived by the utterances of all the authorities he had around him. So is explained the necessity of his "wish."

He proves nothing but himself, his sole proof is himself, all his opponents overcome him at once but not by refuting him (he is irrefutable), but by proving themselves.

Human associations rest on this, that someone by superior force of life gives the appearance of having refuted other individuals in themselves irrefutable. The result is sweet and comforting for those individuals, but it is deficient in truth and invariably therefore in permanence.

He was once part of a monumental group. Around some elevated figure or other in the center were ranged in carefully thought-out order symbolical images of the military caste, the arts, the sciences, the handicrafts. He was one of those many figures. Now the group is long since dispersed, or at least he has left it and makes his way through life alone. He no longer has even his old vocation, indeed he has actually forgotten what he once represented. Probably it is this very forgetting that gives rise to a certain melancholy, uncertainty, unrest, a certain longing for vanished ages, darkening the present. And yet this longing is an essential element in human effort, perhaps indeed human effort itself.

He does not live for the sake of his personal life; he does not think for the sake of his personal thoughts. It seems to him that he lives and thinks under the compulsion of a family, which, it is true, is itself superabundant in life and thought, but for which he constitutes, in obedience to some law unknown to him, a formal necessity. Because of this unknown family and this unknown law he cannot be exempted.

The original sin, the ancient wrong committed by man, consists in the complaint, which man makes and never ceases making, that a wrong has been done to him, that the original sin was once committed upon him.

Two children were loitering beside Casinelli's shop window, a boy of about six, a girl of seven, both well dressed; they were talking of God and sin. I stopped behind them. The girl, who seemed to be a Catholic, held that the only real sin was to deceive God. With childish obstinacy the boy, who seemed to be a Protestant, asked what, then, it was to deceive human beings or to steal. "That's a very great sin too," said the girl "but not the greatest, the greatest sins are those against God; for sins against human beings we have the confessional. When I confess the angel again stands behind me in an instant, for when I commit a sin the devil comes behind me, only I don't see him." And tired of being half in earnest, she spun around light-heartedly on her heel and said: "Look, there's nobody behind me." The boy spun around too and saw me there. "Look," he said, without considering that I must hear him, or perhaps without caring, "the devil is standing behind me." "I see him too," replied the girl, "but that's not the one I meant."

He does not want consolation, yet not because he does not want it—who does not want it?—but because to seek for consolation would mean to devote his whole life to the task, to live perpetually on the very frontiers of his existence, almost outside it, barely knowing for whom he was seeking consolation, and consequently not even capable of finding effective consolation, effective, not real consolation, for real consolation does not exist.

He fights against having his limits defined by his fellow men. No man, even if he be infallible, can see more than that fraction of his neighbor for which his strength and kind of vision are adapted. He has, however, like everybody, but in its most extreme form, the longing to limit himself to the limit of his neighbor's eyesight. Had Robinson Crusoe never left the highest, or, more correctly, the most visible point of his island, from desire for comfort, or timidity, or fear, or ignorance, or longing, he would soon have perished; but since without paying any attention to passing ships and their feeble telescopes he started to explore the whole island and take pleasure in it, he managed to keep himself alive and finally was found after all, by a chain of causality that was, of course, logically inevitable.

"You make a virtue of your necessity."

"In the first place everyone does that, and in the second, that's just what I don't do. I let my necessity remain necessity. I do not drain the swamp, but live in its feverish exhalations."

"That's the very thing you make a virtue of."

"Like everyone, as I said before. But I only do it for your sake. I take injury to my soul that you may remain friendly to me."

Everything is allowed him, except self-oblivion, wherewith, however, everything in turn is denied him, except the one thing necessary at the given moment for the whole.

The question of conscience is a social imposition. All virtues are individual, all vices social. The things that pass as social virtues, love, for example, disinterestedness, justice, self-sacrifice, are only "astonishingly" enfeebled social vices.

The difference between the "Yes" and "No" that he says to his contemporaries and those that he should actually say, might be likened to the difference between life and death, and is just as vaguely divined by him.

The reason why posterity's judgment of individuals is juster than the contemporary one lies in their being dead. One develops in one's own style only after death, only when one is alone. Death is to the individual like Saturday evening to the chimney sweep; it washes the dirt from his body. Then it can be seen whether his contemporaries harmed him more, or whether he did the more harm to his contemporaries; in the latter case he was a great man.

The strength to deny, that most natural expression of the perpetually changing, renewing, dying, reviving human fighting organism, we possess always, but not the courage, although life is denial, and therefore denial affirmation.

He does not die along with his dying thoughts. Dying is merely a phenomenon within the inner world (which remains intact, even if it too should be only an idea), a natural phenomenon like any other, neither happy nor sad.

The current against which he swims is so rapid that in certain absent moods he is sometimes cast into despair by the blank peace amid which he splashes, so infinitely far has he been driven back in a moment of surrender.

He is thirsty, and is cut off from a spring by a mere dump of bushes. But he is divided against himself: one part overlooks the whole, sees that he is standing here and that the spring is just beside him; but another part notices nothing, has at most a divination that the first part sees all. But as he notices nothing he cannot drink.

He is neither bold nor rash. But neither is he fearful. A free life would not alarm him. Now he has never been granted such a life, but that too causes him no anxiety, for he has no anxiety of any kind about himself. There exists, however, a Someone completely unknown to him, who has a great and continuous anxiety for him—for him alone. This anxiety of this Someone concerning him, and in particular the continuousness of this anxiety, sometimes causes him torturing head-aches in his quieter hours.

A certain heaviness, a feeling of being secured against every vicissitude, the vague assurance of a bed prepared for him and belonging to him alone, keeps him from getting up; but he is kept from lying still by an unrest which drives him from his bed, by his conscience, the endless beating of his heart, the fear of death and the longing to refute it: all this will not let him rest and he gets up again. This up and down and a few fortuitous, desultory, irrelevant observations made in the course of it, are his life.

He has two antagonists: The first pushes him from behind, from his origin. The second blocks his road ahead. He struggles with both. Actually the first supports him in his struggle with the second, for the first wants to push him forward; and in the same way the second supports him in his struggle with the first; for the second of course forces him back. But it is only theoretically so. For it is not only the two protagonists who are there, but he himself as well, and who really knows his intentions? However that may be, he has

a dream that sometime in an unguarded moment—
it would require, though, a night as dark as no night
has ever been—he will spring out of the fighting line
and be promoted, on account of his experience of such
warfare, as judge over his struggling antagonists.

THE SCHOCKEN KAFKA LIBRARY

AMERIKA
a new translation by Mark Harman, based on the restored text

Kafka's first and funniest novel tells the story of the young immigrant Karl Rossmann, who, "packed off to America" by his parents, finds himself caught up in a whirlwind of dizzying reversals, strange escapades, and picaresque adventures.

"Almost ninety years after his death, Kafka continues to defy simplifications, to force us to consider him anew. That's the effect of Mark Harman's new translation."
—*Los Angeles Times*

APHORISMS
foreword by Daniel Frank

Appearing for the first time in a single volume, all the aphorisms penned by Kafka during two significant periods in his life.

"If there is a theology in Kafka, this is the only place where he himself comes close to declaring it."
—Roberto Calasso

THE CASTLE
a new translation by Mark Harman, based on the restored text

This haunting tale of a man known only as K. and his endless struggle against an inscrutable authority to gain admittance to a castle is often cited as Kafka's most autobiographical work.

"Will be *the* translation of preference for some time to come."
— J. M. Coetzee, *The New York Review of Books*

THE COMPLETE STORIES
edited by Nahum N. Glatzer, with a foreword by John Updike

All of Kafka's stories are collected here in one comprehensive volume; with the exception of the three novels, the whole of his narrative work is included.

"The Complete Stories is an encyclopedia of our insecurities and our brave attempts to oppose them."
— Anatole Broyard

DIARIES, 1910–1923
edited by Max Brod

For the first time in this country, the complete diaries of Franz Kafka are available in one volume. Covering the period from 1910 to 1923, the year before Kafka's death, they reveal the essential Kafka behind the enigmatic artist.

"It is likely that these journals will be regarded as one of [Kafka's] major literary works; in these pages, he reveals what he customarily hid from the world."
— *The New Yorker*

LETTER TO HIS FATHER
bilingual edition, with an introduction by Tom McCarthy

Kafka's poignant letter to Hermann Kafka, written in 1919 but never delivered, locates the tragic gulf between father and son within the larger existential dilemma that informed so much of his work.

"Kafka's principal attempt at self-clarification is also one of the great confessions of literature."
F. W. Dupee, *The New York Times Book Review*

LETTERS TO MILENA
translated and with an introduction by Philip Boehm

In no other work does Kafka reveal himself as in this collection of letters to Milena Jesenská, his twenty-three-year-old Czech translator. A business correspondence that developed into a passionate but doomed epistolary love affair with a woman he described as "a living fire, such as I have never seen," it shows us a Kafka not seen in any of his other writings.

"Kafka's voice here is more personal, more pure, and more painful than in his fiction: a testimony to human existence, and to our eternal wait for the impossible."
—Jan Kott

THE METAMORPHOSIS AND OTHER STORIES
translated by Willa and Edwin Muir

This powerful collection brings together all the stories Franz Kafka published during his lifetime, including "The Judgment," "The Metamorphosis," "In the Penal Colony," "A Country Doctor," and "A Hunger Artist."

"Kafka's survey of the insectile situation of young Jews in inner Bohemia can hardly be improved upon. There is a sense in which Kafka's Jewish question has become everybody's question, Jewish alienation the template for all our doubts. These days we all find our anterior legs flailing before us. We're all insects, all *Ungeziefer,* now."
—Zadie Smith

THE SONS

translations revised and updated by Arthur Wensinger,
with an introduction by Mark Anderson

Franz Kafka's three classic stories of filial revolt—"The Metamorphosis," "The Judgment," and "The Stoker"— grouped together with his own poignant "Letter to His Father," take on fresh, compelling meaning.

"Kafka is the author who comes nearest to bearing the same kind of relationship to our age as Dante, Shakespeare, and Goethe bore to theirs."   —W. H. Auden

THE TRIAL

a new translation by Breon Mitchell,
based on the restored text

The terrifying story of Joseph K., his arrest and trial, is one of the greatest novels of the twentieth century.

"Mitchell's translation is an accomplishment of the highest order—one that will honor Kafka far into the twenty-first century."
                    —Walter Abish, author of *How German Is It*